IGNITE

EMPOWERING WOMEN TO HEAL, ACHIEVE, AND SUCCEED

SHANNON DeGARMO

Nashville, Tennessee

Ignite: Empowering Women to Heal, Achieve, and Succeed
© 2019 by Shannon DeGarmo

All rights reserved. No portion of this book may be reproduced, stored in a retrieval system, or transmitted in any form or bey any means—electronic, mechanical, photocopy, recording, scanning, or other—except for brief quotations in critical reviews or articles, without the proper written permission of the author.

Shannon DeGarmo is represented by Ambassador Speakers, Inc.
Phone: 615-370-4700 or website: www.ambassadorspeakers.com

Unless otherwise noted, all Scripture quotations are taken from THE HOLY BIBLE, NEW INTERNATIONAL VERSION®, NIV® Copyright © 1973, 1978, 1984, 2011 by Biblica, Inc.® Used by permission. All rights reserved worldwide.

Scripture quotations marked isv are taken from *The Holy Bible: International Standard Version*. Release 2.0, Build 2015.02.09. Copyright © 1995-2014 by ISV Foundation. ALL RIGHTS RESERVED INTERNATIONALLY. Used by permission of Davidson Press, LLC.

ISBN-978-1-7327417-2-0

Cappella Books
P.O. Box 50358, Nashville, TN 37205

Printed in the United States of America

To those of us who need another chance.

This is a beautiful beginning.

Contents

Introduction / *1*

Commitment Statement / *3*

Section 1: Achieve and Succeed / *5*

    Chapter 1.   Finding Strengths: Aptitude Test / *7*

    Chapter 2.   Creating a Life Mission Statement / *13*

    Chapter 3.   Importance of Setting Goals / *19*

    Chapter 4.   Writing a Résumé / *23*

    Chapter 5.   Getting a Job / *31*

    Chapter 6.   The Meaning of Sacrifice: Needs vs. Wants / *37*

Section 2: Heal / *45*

    Chapter 7.   Who Am I?: Exploring Self-Worth / *47*

    Chapter 8.   Identifying Coping Strategies / *55*

    Chapter 9.   The Power of Regret / *59*

    Chapter 10.   The Forgiveness Process / *65*

    Chapter 11.   Creating a Support System / *71*

Section 3: Lesson Plans / *75*

Ignite

Introduction

Before you jump right into this workbook, it's good to know what you're getting into. *Ignite* is designed to supplement your success, not only in your career choice, but also as an individual. This faith-based program gives you tools to realize your value and purpose in Christ, move toward healthier life choices, and reach your personal goals to fulfill your potential. Oh, the places you're gonna go!

With *Ignite*, you will become part of a network of people who are willing to walk with you on your journey. Many of them have similar stories of hardship and want to celebrate with others (like you) as they overcome life's circumstances. *Ignite* is intended to create a community where support and encouragement are found when making decisions such as continuing your education, getting your finances in order, parenting—whatever phase you find yourself in.

Ignite believes that the Bible is absolute truth. As a group, its members depend on God's Word to find guidance, healing, and wholeness. Along with practical resources and reflective activities, we believe that faith is foundational to individual growth and moving forward in life.

Take a deep breath! Look around you at others who are choosing to take this journey with you. These are your people; this is your tribe. Just as iron sharpens iron, you will encourage one another in your goals. There will be times you will speak wisdom to, cry with, laugh with, and celebrate one another's victories. In other words, you will be like a family.

Ignite is only the first step. As with everything, it is good to continue your growth through Christian counseling, church attendance, and other small group gatherings.

I am so honored that you are allowing me to be part of your stories. I can't wait to see the beauty that will come from ashes . . . even the most beautiful flowers can bloom in the desert.

This is the beginning of something amazing!
God Bless

Shannon DeGarmo

Ignite

Commitment Statement

Being part of something bigger than you takes dedication and commitment. To fully be engaged in this process and to get the most out of it, there needs to be some "ground rules"—a foundation based on expectations so the program can be as impactful as possible.

Don't worry, this is not a contract. However, it is a commitment (a promise) about moving forward as an individual and how to treat yourself and others in the group. These are guidelines that promote spiritual, emotional, physical health and growth. They are pivotal to success within the program.

- **Come as you are**. There is no need to pretend to be anything else but you. No matter what brought you to this group, everyone's story connects each of us through some form of brokenness. It's OK. Embrace the freedom that comes with transparency.
- **What is said within the group stays within the group.** We need our "family" to be a safe place. To do that, we need to know that our vulnerabilities and our insecurities are being protected by one another. We are not to gossip or share with anyone or use any intimate information against another person.
- **Listen without judging**. We have all walked different paths and have different backgrounds, but pain feels the same to everyone. This program is the beginning of something new. We are meant to learn from our past and not be defined by it.
- **Boys stay on the side (unless you are in a committed, stable relationship).** This is a time for you. To grow and reflect on your goals, you've got to focus on yourself. Dating can distract from what the Lord wants to work in you. Dating will come, but at a better time and place.

- **Honesty is what works.** To get the most out of any kind of change, it's vital to be honest—with those around you and, more importantly, with yourself. This will be a time to push yourself to think about the "whys" of your life and who you want to be. The more you reflect honestly about your choices, the better your choices will be.
- **Don't quit.** You can be discouraged, you can be annoyed, but promise yourself not to quit. Changing is not easy—if it were, everyone would do it more often. Encourage one another when the road gets difficult.
- **Expect to fail, but not stay there.** Success is a journey that includes failure. It's OK to mess up. But we need to own our mess, learn from it, and move on.
- **Pray.** Commit to praying for guidance, patience, stamina—for yourself and for one another. The Lord is willing to meet us where we are now and lead us to where He wants us to be. He is faithful.

Signature   *Date*

Section 1: Achieve and Succeed

*These lessons are designed to support you
in your personal achievement and guide you toward success.*

Finding Strengths Objectives:
- Understanding the importance of personal gifts
- Complete the Personality Profiler Test
- Analyze the results
- Discuss and decide on a plan to further education or career choices

Creating a Life Mission Statement Objectives:
- Understand the benefits of a Life Mission Statement
- Analyze personal goals and direction in life
- Create a personal Life Mission Statement

Importance of Setting Goals Objectives:
- Understand the benefits of having personal goals
- Decide on three reachable goals
- Create a goal "road map" that is an individual plan for how to achieve set goals

Writing a Résumé Objectives:
- Become familiar with the different parts of a résumé and the overall goal in writing one
- Identify personal skills and past experiences to include
- Create a rough draft résumé and, ultimately, a final document

Getting a Job Objectives:

- Learn basic job interview etiquette
- Understand appropriate job interview attire
- Learn how to properly give a handshake
- Discuss personal responses to job interview questions
- Participate in mock job interview

Needs Vs. Wants Objectives:

- Distinguish between a need and a want
- Analyze personal spending habits
- Create a personal budget

Chapter 1

Finding Strengths: Aptitude Test

*We have different gifts, according to the grace given to each of us.
If your gift is prophesying, then prophesy in accordance with your faith;
if it is serving, then serve; if it is teaching, then teach; if it is to encourage,
then give encouragement; if it is giving, then give generously;
if it is to lead, do it diligently; if it is to show mercy, do it cheerfully.*

—Romans 12:3–8

We *all* have strengths . . . even if we can't see or recognize them. The Lord has graciously given each of us special abilities to develop and use for His purposes. We didn't do anything to deserve them—they are gifts. However, not using our gifts is like going through life in a fog . . . Like choosing to live in a gray cloud when we could be living in a world with a million colors all around.

Some of our strengths I consider "loud" strengths. These are the ones that the world makes a big fuss over, like athleticism, artistic ability, or a genius IQ. These are the ones that bring applause and notoriety. But there are hundreds of other strengths—the steady and "quiet" ones that usually come with adversity. Empathy, perseverance, and integrity are not something we can see on the outside of a person. These strengths are embedded in our spirits and connected to our DNA. They usually lay sleeping until a bump in the road comes along and shakes them to the surface. Not until then do we see how these God-given gifts become so valuable.

Being able to use our gifts, not only in life's struggles, but also in our career choices, brings such purpose. We all like to do things we are good at, but how do we know what our gifts are and what careers will benefit from them? Hold on because you are about to find out.

LESSON NOTES

LESSON NOTES

Quotes of Strength

"If you don't like the road you're walking, start paving another one." —*Dolly Parton*

"You can't give up! If you give up, you're like everybody else." —*Chris Evert*

"The tests we face in life's journey are not to reveal our weaknesses, but to help us discover our inner strengths. We can only know how strong we are when we strive and thrive beyond the challenges we face." —*Kemi Sogunle*

"You may encounter many defeats, but you must not be defeated. In fact it may be necessary to encounter the defeats so you can know who you are and what you can rise from, how you can still come out of it." —*Maya Angelou*

Career/Educational Mapping

STRENGTHS

AREAS OF STUDY

TOP 4 JOBS

How to Get There

- **EDUCATION**
- **FINANCIAL**
- **SUPPORT**
- **TIMELINE**
- **FINISH LINE**

Chapter 2

Creating a Life Mission Statement

*The purpose of life is not to be happy. It is to be useful,
to be honorable, to be compassionate, to have it make some difference
that you have lived and lived well.*

—Ralph Waldo Emerson

Going through life without purpose is almost like being a leaf being carried by a breeze—it floats aimlessly and without direction. Sometimes, because of difficult circumstances, life can be that way. But it doesn't have to stay that way—it's not meant to be a permanent address to live. Thing is, we all have a purpose. Just like our curly hair or crooked toe, we are born with one. Some people discover their purpose early on. It's as though they have clear focus and direction without even trying. Others of us, it takes some time and reflection to figure it out. We need time to understand who we are just the way God made us to be.

Defining our purpose gives us, well, more purpose. We have an overriding theme in our life that we choose to live by—it's a theme we are driven by. We know why we are on the planet, what we want to do while living on it, and what kind of legacy we want to leave. Purpose gives us focus, guidance, and meaning. It allows us to jump off the crazy breeze that's carrying us and move where God directs us to go.

Make sure you've got on comfy shoes, because we are about to begin walking with purpose.

LESSON NOTES

LESSON NOTES

Personal Life Mission Statements

♦ *"I define personal success as being consistent to my own personal mission statement: To love God and love others."* —Joel Manby (owns family oriented entertainment organizations like Dollywood and Harlem Globetrotters)

♦ *"To serve as a leader, live a balanced life, and apply ethical principles to make a significant difference."* —Denise Morrison, CEO Campbell's Soup Company

♦ *"To glorify God by being a faithful steward of all that is entrusted to us. To have a positive influence on all who come in contact with Chick-fil-A."* (business mission statement)

Creating a Life Mission Statement 17

Biblical Mission Statements

♦ *Therefore go and make disciples of all Nations, baptizing them in the name of the Father and of the Son and of the Holy Spirit, and teaching them to obey everything I have commanded you. And surely I am with you always, to the very end of the age.*
—Matthew 28:19-20

♦ *For this is what the Lord has commanded us: "I have made you a light for the Gentiles, that you may bring salvation to the ends of the earth."* —Acts 13:14

♦ *He said to them, "Go into all the world and preach the gospel to all creation."* —Mark 16:15

♦ *Everyone who calls on the name of the Lord will be saved." How, then can they call the one they have not believed in? And how can they believe in the one of whom they have not heard? And how can they hear without someone preaching to them?*
—Romans 10:13-14

♦ *And the gospel must first be preached to all nations.* —Mark 13:10

notes

My Life Mission Statement

- Look to the Bible and guidance from Jesus. We are told that we are created to glorify the Lord (*everyone who is called by my name, whom I created for my glory, whom I formed and made —Isaiah 43:7*) So, if we are walking in Christ, your mission statement should include Him and His plans for us.

- Include your personal gifts (if you love to teach, serve or volunteer, your mission statement should include that).

- Think about your future self, who do you want to be?

- Include your legacy goals (what do you want people to remember you as).

your mission statement

Chapter 3

Importance of Setting Goals

*Greatness is not measured by what a man or woman accomplishes,
but by the opposition he or she has overcome to reach his goals.*
—Dorothy Height

It is so easy to get lost in the everyday things. Routines can literally take over, and before we know it, years have gone by without having realized any personal goals. Unless we live our lives intentionally, we will wake up one morning discovering that we accomplished very little of what we dreamed. Remember those—the dreams that used to make your heart flutter? The ones where you could be whatever or whoever you wanted to be? Do you still have them or have they gotten buried under the busyness and demands?

Dreams are important. They give us the ability to see what we can become. They give us freedom without boundaries. But we can't just wish and dream if we want to actually accomplish our goals. We can't just pray to become a doctor—we also have to put in the time, work, and sacrifice to earn that title. Catch my drift?

Because of where we are in our lives, sometimes we can think our dreams are dead. Our lives are too busy, screwed up, or our responsibilities are too great even to dare to dream. Thing is, that's just not true. We talk ourselves out of our dreams because we think the work is too much, or it's impossible to reach because of _____. Here's the deal, we don't get over a mountain in one jump. That's impossible. We take a lot of little steps to get there. That's where our goals come in. They are the little steps that we achieve one at a time to get us to the top of that mountain. The more steps you achieve, the more confidence you get. And before you know it, you're running.

LESSON NOTES

LESSON NOTES

22 IGNITE

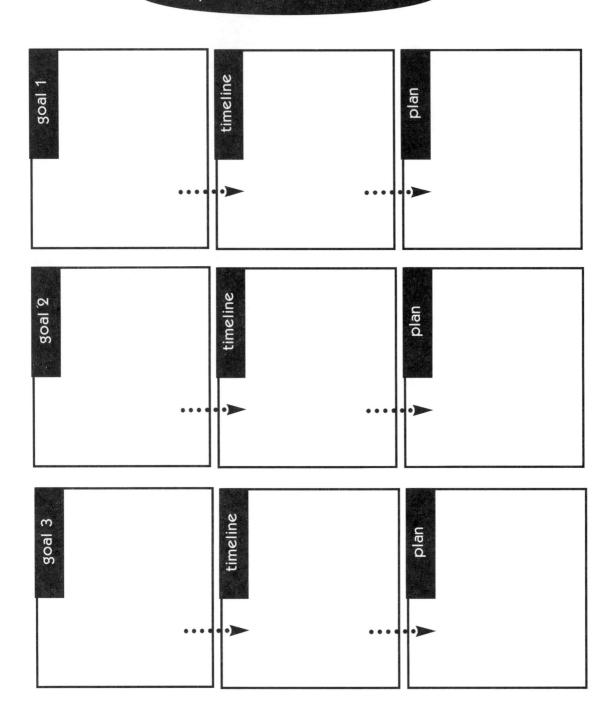

Chapter 4

Writing a Résumé

*Life is what happens when you're making other plans.
So does your résumé. It takes on a life of its own if you let it.
Some people try to map out their paths and plan every step,
but in reality, life hands you something better.
A dead end is really a detour to a new route you hadn't planned on taking.
Every experience enhances your life now or later.*

—Regina Brett

A résumé. It's a sheet of paper that reveals a glimpse into who we are, what we have done, and what we are doing now. If you look at it one way, a résumé is a reminder of our failures and lack of experience. If that thought comes into your head, squish it away like a summertime fly. Failures are merely opportunities to learn, and any experience has the potential to grow us. Job experience is one thing, but life experience is something totally different. Don't discount *any* experiences you've had—it's all important. Our past life experience is always preparing us for our future perfect job.

We all have something to offer. Be proud of where you've come from and be positive about where you are going.

LESSON NOTES

LESSON NOTES

Résumé Rules

- Always include your contact information. How else is an employer going to find you if they can't get in touch with you?

- Don't lie—it's *never* okay to lie. Employers run background checks and call references. If you lie, it's a perfect way *never* to get hired.

- Don't include any unnecessary information such as your marital status, hobbies, or social media tags. Employers will look up your social media sites. On that note: please make sure they all have appropriate language and photos!

- Don't write down a salary on your résumé. Money is to be discussed in the interview.

- Don't complain about a former employer. For example, "I left because my old boss was very difficult to work with." It puts you in a bad light and could possibly make a future employer nervous about hiring you.

- Create a professional email address. Professional email addresses usually include your first and last name (or last initial). We don't want to put iheartcats@gmail.com on a professional résumé.

- Always have a good friend look it over to check for grammar and spelling errors. Let them give honest feedback for making it better. They may find something you missed, or they may have a great idea for you to include.

Résumé Example

Shannon DeGarmo
(address)
(town)
(professional email address)
(phone)

"It is the supreme art of the teacher to awaken joy
in creative expression and knowledge." —Albert Einstein

Career Objective

A teaching position that nourishes the emotional, spiritual, and educational development of children.

Education

Middle Tennessee State University
1301 East Main Street
Murfreesboro, TN 37132

*Undergraduate Degree: Bachelor's of Science in Elementary Education (2006)

Middle Tennessee State University

*Master's Degree of Education in Administration and Supervision K-12 Schools (2012)

Honors

*Member of National Society of Collegiate Scholars

*Dean's List six semesters

*Cumulative GPA 3.7 (Undergraduate) and Cumulative GPA 3.9 (Graduate)

*Phi Kappa Phi Honors Society

Experience

2011- Current: Fifth- and Sixth-Grade Instructor at Ironwood Academy

- Taught Composition, Literature, and Social Studies to homeschoolers
- Participated in parent-teacher conferences
- Created curriculum mapping for Tennessee Academic Standards and National Core Curriculum Standards for my particular subjects
- Participated and completed all duties and responsibilities for Ironwood Instructor (faculty meetings, communication with parents, completing grades)
- Created original lesson plans that adhere to Tennessee Academic Standards and National Core Curriculum Standards

2006-2009 Fifth-Grade Elementary School Teacher for Winstead Elementary in Franklin, TN

- Highly qualified to teach K-6
- Taught Language Arts, Social Studies, and Math
- Love and Logic representative for the school
- Created monthly presentations for faculty
- Participated in Roger Taylor's three-day training of integrated units of study
- Destination Imagination club leader for Winstead

Résumé Example, cont.

- Geography Club leader for Winstead
- Create original lesson plans that follow Tennessee Academic Standards
- Created newsletters for fifth-grade level
- Enjoyed collaborating with teachers for higher level thinking among students
- Effectively worked with administration and team for the education of the children
- Worked closely with technology coach to learn Photoshop and Movie Maker programs

Skills and Interest

- Valid Tennessee teacher's license
- Valid administrative license
- Proficient in Word, Excel, PowerPoint, Photoshop, and Internet research
- Educated in the Tennessee Coordinated School Health program
- Educated in Michigan Model Curriculum
- Basic Spanish speaking, writing, and reading skills
- Published songwriter
- Passionate about the arts
- Being involved in the education of children

Create Your Own Résumé

Name

Address

Email Address

Phone

Quote

Career Objective

Education

Employment History

Skills & Interest

References

Chapter 5

Getting a Job

Whatever you do, work at it with all your heart, as working for the Lord, not for human masters, since you know that you will receive an inheritance from the Lord as a reward. It is the Lord Christ you are serving.

—Colossians 3:23–24

There are jobs we love, there are jobs we hate, and there are jobs we love to hate. Throughout our life, we usually have many different jobs that fall anywhere from one end of the love/hate scale to the other. Some jobs are born of need, some we have because we want to do them, and some we take for a season because they're a stepping stone to the next one. That's okay. There is honor in any kind of work (as long as it is moral and not illegal).

If we are working toward our goals and Life Mission Statement, we aren't necessarily where we want to be in our careers yet. That means we may have to work jobs that aren't our "dream" jobs. These are our "in-between" jobs where we know it's not forever. It's a pit stop, but it shouldn't change the way we work—and that is with excellence. In any job, we are working for the Lord, and we are to give it our all. Whether mopping floors, cleaning dishes, or flipping burgers, we do it with a heart that reflects His glory. Paying dues in the pit stops is just part of the process. We start out at the bottom and work our way up knowing that each step is headed toward that dream job.

LESSON NOTES

LESSON NOTES

Handshake Rules

1. Handshakes are with the right hand unless there is a disability.

2. If you are about to meet someone, make sure your right hand is free. For example, if you are carrying a folder, put it in your left hand.

3. Walk in with your hands free, not in your pockets. It expresses openness.

4. Extend your right hand while making eye contact.

5. The handshake should be firm (about as firm as the other person's).

6. You should shake hands up and down about 2-3 times.

7. Express a greeting like, "Hello," or "Good Afternoon."

8. Introduce yourself by saying your first and last name.

9. Say "Nice to meet you," or "Thank you for having me."

10. If you are sitting when someone comes in, stand up and shake hands. THINGS TO AVOID: The Dead Fish handshake, sweaty palms, or clammy hands.

Do's and Don'ts Attire

Job Interview

1. Do wear something comfortable.

2. Do wear your hair in a way that's presentable. (Down or pulled back out of your face).

3. Do wear pants or a dress.

4. Do wear a blouse or sweater.

5. Do wear make-up that is muted and subtle.

6. Do sit up straight (and cross those ankles or legs if you are wearing a skirt).

• •

1. Don't wear halter tops, tank tops, shorts, sleeveless shirts or mini-skirts.

2. Don't wear extreme make-up that can be distracting.

3. Don't wear flip-flops or opened-toed sandals.

4. Don't wear a ponytail, a distracting hat, or hair accessory.

5. Don't wear jewelry that makes noise.

6. Don't have your cell phone out where anyone can see. Turn it off and put it away.

Mock Job Interview

Personal Interview Response

1. What are my strengths (in relation to the job I'm applying for).

2. What kind of job experience do I already have?

3. What is my plan to further myself, i.e. education, volunteering, etc.

4. What skills do I already have that I can bring to a job?

5. Why would I make a good candidate for a job?

Job Interview Questions

1. Tell me something about yourself.

2. What's something you feel confident about?

3. What's something you are working on?

4. Would you describe yourself as dependable? Why?

5. Are you willing to learn a new skill? How quickly do you learn?

6. What makes you different from others?

7. What motivates you?

8. Describe yourself.

9. How do you handle failure?

10. Tell me about your job experience.

Chapter 6

The Meaning of Sacrifice: Needs vs. Wants

"Do not worry, saying, 'What shall we eat?' or 'What shall we drink?' or 'What shall we wear?' For the pagans run after all these things, and your heavenly Father knows that you need them. But seek first his kingdom and his righteousness, and all these things will be given to you as well. Therefore do not worry about tomorrow, for tomorrow will worry about itself. Each day has enough trouble of it's own."

—Matthew 6:31–34

"Y'all, that new phone came out yesterday and I just *have* to have it. Like, I will literally die without it," said *me*! How many times have we told ourselves that we *need* something that we really *want*? We spend so much time, energy, and money on *things*. That's right…plain ole things that bring temporary happiness and, many times, guilt with the price tag.

In reality, we don't need a whole lot. Everything that we need, God has promised to provide. Yet, we still act like the gerbil inside the plastic ball running and going nowhere trying to accumulate stuff.

Understanding the basic difference between a need and a want can free you from that spending/regret cycle. Being able to save for an emergency, school, or even a trip brings such a sense of accomplishment that you are working toward something instead of trying to just stay afloat.

So, next time you walk past that window with the amazing shoes, keep on walking because instead of running and going nowhere in that plastic ball, you're actually going to go places.

LESSON NOTES

LESSON NOTES

Everyday Life

• Circle what you think you *need* on a regular basis
(2 or 3 times a month)

movies • lunch out • breakfast out • dinner out • new phone • app subscriptions • car maintenance • jewelry • hair color • Starbucks • manicures • pedicures • make-up • diapers • groceries • medicine • facials • cable • rent/mortgage • car payment • cigarettes (includes vape and other types of smoking) • school supplies • utilities • internet • pets • gas • alcohol • shoes • lottery tickets • designer clothes • soda • formula • children's clothes • credit card payment • tuition • bus fare • video games • Redbox • Hulu • ice cream • candy • toilet paper • shampoo • health insurance • iTunes • car insurance • phone bill • massages • toothpaste • bottled water • milk • pet food/supplies

Needs List

These are the things that you *really need* to survive:

- Food (from the store that you make at home)
- Water (milk and formula too)
- Shelter (including utilities: heat/air, electricity)
- Clothing (not designer clothing)
- Medical care
- Toiletries (toothpaste, toilet paper, feminine products)
- Phone that works
- Transportation

notes

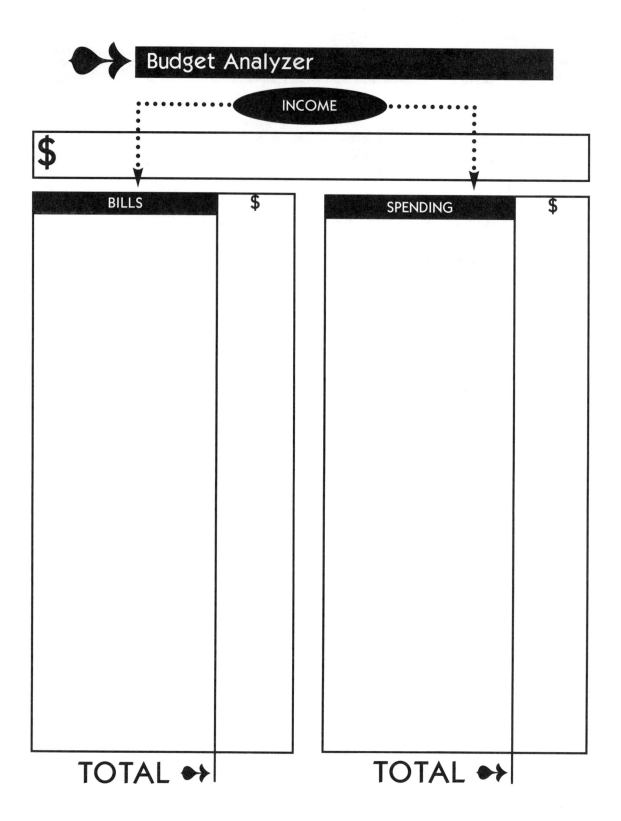

This or That

Example

THIS IS WHAT I DO	WHEN I CAN DO THAT
pay for a manicure	have a manicure party with friends

THIS	THAT

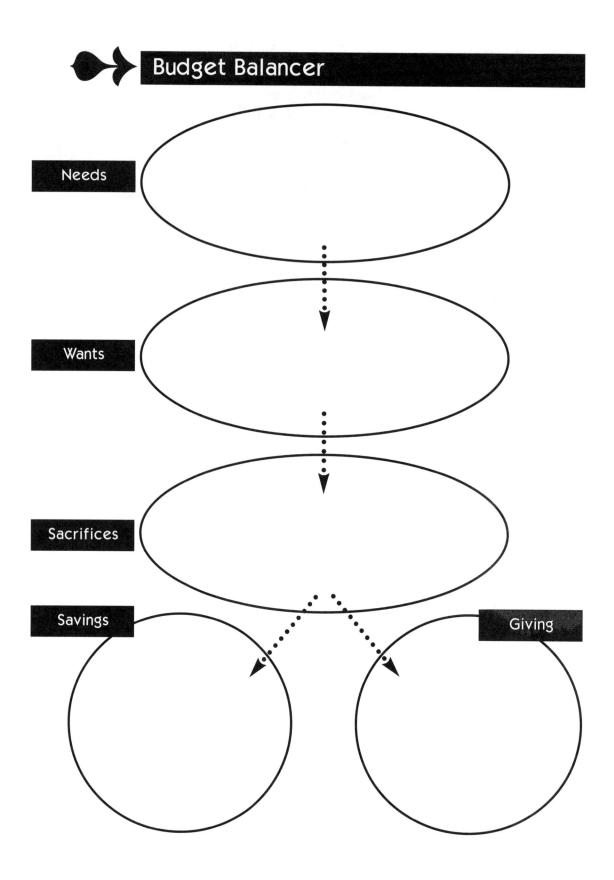

Section 2: Heal

These lessons are designed to support you in personal reflection and discovery, become comfortable with your authentic self, and move toward a future filled with healthy decisions and a positive self-image.

Who Am I? Exploring Self-Worth Objectives:

- Identify positive self-worth statements vs. negative self-harmful statements
- Analyze self-worth from a personal perspective
- Learn how to use positive affirmation statements
- Explore how we allow others to influence our self-worth
- Understand that self-worth is given to us by God

Identifying Coping Strategies Objectives:

- Identify how trauma causes an effect on our lives
- Analyze personal feelings around trauma
- Identify individual coping mechanisms and their effect on our lives
- Understand the difference between healthy and unhealthy coping strategies

Power of Regret Objectives:

- Define regret
- Identify regret as a valuable tool
- Analyze personal regret
- Acknowledge what personal opportunities are born from regret

The Forgiveness Process Objectives:

- Identify any pain and resentment
- Understand what forgiveness is and its purpose
- Identify any people or circumstances that forgiveness is being withheld
- Begin the forgiveness process

Creating A Support System Objectives:
- Identify qualities of good friendships
- Understand that balance is important in friendship
- Identify qualities of those in a support system
- Identify the benefits of a support system
- Create a usable support system

Chapter 7

Who Am I?: Exploring Self-Worth

Be yourself, everyone else is taken.
—Oscar Wilde

Who we are is not defined by what we've done. Who we are is defined by Christ: "For we are God's handiwork, created in Christ Jesus to do good works, which God prepared in advance for us to do" Ephesians 2:10. However, we can have a tendency to allow others to cloud our view of our self-worth. Over time, the cloud can take control and we can't even see our own reflections anymore. All we see is a culmination of our past and become convinced that others determine our value. Many times, focusing on our past is suffocating. And it's so easy to lose our identity there. Our brains get on "auto-pilot" mode and continually repeat a vicious cycle of what others have told us we are, and the truth of who God says we are gets lost.

However, there's good news, girls. Just like everyone has unique fingerprints, we all have a unique spirit created by a heavenly Father who sees our hearts and knows our thoughts. There is nothing He can't overcome, and there is nothing that shocks Him. We aren't too far gone, too damaged, too abused, or too addicted. We are His daughters, and He sees beyond our past. He sees our potential.

Understanding ourselves is not an easy road. As with all journeys, it starts with one step. And each step is a good one! Hold on, you are about to discover one of your greatest gifts . . . *you.*

LESSON NOTES

LESSON NOTES

"I Am" Scripture References

Capable

• Being confident of this, that he who began a good work in you will carry it on to completion until the day of Christ Jesus. —Philippians 1:6

• For the Spirit God gave us does not make us timid, but gives us power, love and self-disipline. —2 Timothy 1:7

• Trust the Lord with all your heart and lean not on our own understanding; in all your ways submit to him, and he will make your paths straight. —Proverbs 3:5-6

• I can do all this through him who gives me strength. —Philippians 4:13

• For the Lord your God is the one who goes with you to fight for you against your enemies to give you victory. —Deuteronomy 20:4

• "For I know the plans I have for you," declares the Lord, "plans to prosper you and not to harm you, plans to give you hope and a future." —Jeremiah 29:11

• She is clothed with strength and dignity; she can laugh at the days to come. —Proverbs 31:25

Self-worth

• Indeed, the very hairs of your head are all numbered. Don't be afraid; you are worth more than many sparrows. —Luke 12:7

• "Do not fear, for I have redeemed you; I have summoned you by name; you are mine." —Isaiah 43:1

• She speaks with wisdom, and faithful instruction is on her tongue. —Proverbs 31:26

• For we are God's handiwork, created in Christ Jesus to do good works, which God prepared in advance for us to do. —Ephesians 2:10

• Your beauty should not come from outward adornment, such as elaborate hairstyles and the wearing of gold jewelry or fine clothes. Rather, it should be that of your own inner self, the unfading beauty of a gentle and quiet spirit, which is of great worth in God's sight. —1 Peter 3:3-4

"I Am" Scripture References, cont.

• By the grace of God I am what I am, and his grace to me was not without effect. No, I worked harder than all of them—yet not I, but the grace of God that was with me. —1 Corinthians 15:10

• Consequently, you are no longer foreigners and strangers, but fellow citizens with God's people and also members of his household, built on the foundation of the apostles and prophets, with Christ Jesus himself as the chief cornerstone. In him the whole building is joined together and rises to become a holy temple in the Lord. And in him you too are being built together to become a dwelling in which God lives by his Spirit. —Ephesians 2:19–22

• I praise you because I am fearfully and wonderfully made; your works are wonderful, I know that full well. —Psalm 139:14

• She is worth far more than rubies. —Proverbs 31:10

• Brothers and sisters, I do not consider myself yet to have taken hold of it. But one thing I do: Forgetting what is behind and straining toward what is ahead, I press on toward the goal to win the prize for which God has called me heavenward in Christ Jesus. —Philippians 3:13–14

• Forget the former things; do not dwell on the past. See, I am doing a new thing! Now it springs up; do you not perceive it? I am making a way in the wilderness and streams in the wasteland. —Isaiah 43:18–19

• Those who look to him are radiant; their faces are never covered with shame. This poor man called, and the Lord heard him; he saved him out of all his troubles. —Psalm 34:5–6

• Do not be afraid; you will not be put to shame. Do not fear disgrace; you will not be humiliated. You will forget the shame of your youth and remember no more the reproach of your widowhood. —Isaiah 54:4

"I Am" Scripture References, cont.

Forgiven

• If we confess our sins, he is faithful and just and will forgive us our sins and purify us from all unrighteousness. —1 John 1:9

• There is now no condemnation for those who are in Christ Jesus, because through Christ Jesus the law of the Spirit who gives life has set you free from the law of sin and death. —Romans 8:1-2

• "Very truly I tell you, whoever hears my word and believes him who sent me has eternal life and will not be judged but has crossed over from death to life." —John 5:24

• For as high as the heavens are above the earth, so great is his love for those who fear him; as far as the east is from the west, so far has he removed our transgressions from us. —Psalm 103:11-12

• If anyone is in Christ, the new creation has come: The old has gone, the new is here! —2 Corinthians 5:17

• In him we have redemption through his blood, the forgiveness of sins, in accordance with the riches of God's grace. —Ephesians 1:7

Loved

• For God so loved the world that he gave his one and only Son, that whoever believes in him shall not perish but have eternal life. —John 3:16

• For I am convinced that neither death nor life, neither angels nor demons, neither the present nor the future, nor any powers, neither height nor depth, nor anything else in all creation, will be able to separate us from the love of God that is in Christ Jesus our Lord. —Romans 8:38-39

• He heals the brokenhearted and binds up their wounds. —Psalm 147:3

• The Lord your God is with you, the Mighty Warrior who saves. He will take great delight in you; in his love he will no longer rebuke you, but will rejoice over you with singing. —Zephaniah 3:17

"I Am" Scripture References, cont.

Loved

• This is how God showed his love among us: He sent his one and only Son into the world that we might live through him. This is love: not that we loved God, but that he loved us and sent his Son as an atoning sacrifice for our sins. Dear friends, since-God so loved us, we also ought to love one another. —1 John 4:9-11

Not Alone

• When you pass through the waters, I will be with you; and when you pass through the rivers, they will not sweep over you. When you walk through the fire, you will not be burned; the flames will not set you ablaze. —Isaiah 43:2

• God is our refuge and strength, an ever-present help in trouble. —Psalm 46:1

• The eternal God is your refuge, and underneath are the everlasting arms. He will drive out your enemies before you, saying, "Destroy them!" —Deuteronomy 33:27

• The LORD makes firm the steps of the one who delights in him; though he may stumble, he will not fall, for the LORD upholds him with his hand. —Psalm 37:23-24

• For all have sinned and fall short of the glory of God. —Romans 3:23

• "I have told you these things, so that in me you may have peace. In this world you will have trouble. But take heart! I have overcome the world." —John 16:33

• God is within her, she will not fall; God will help her at break of day. —Psalm 46:5

• The LORD will fight for you; you need only to be still. —Exodus 14:14

Chapter 8

Identifying Coping Strategies

*The depth of the feeling continued to surprise and threaten me,
but each time it hit again and I bore it . . .
I would discover that it hadn't washed me away.*

—Anne Lamott

Why do I keep making the same mistakes? Why do I keep doing things I know I shouldn't? Why can't I stop making the same bad choice? When we are working toward healing, it's important to ask ourselves these types of questions. Many of us go through life repeating poor choices and never really think about how we got to where we are. But, to truly understand the *whys* of what we do, we've got to hit the pause button on the cycles and take some time to look at our past.

Digging deep into our past can be scary. There may be places that haven't seen the light in a long time. However, understanding and embracing our past helps us develop our future, which is so important for healing. Our memories are memories. We can use them as an excuse to drown us, or we can use them as a reason to move forwards. The choice is always yours.

LESSON NOTES

LESSON NOTES

Identifying Coping Strategies

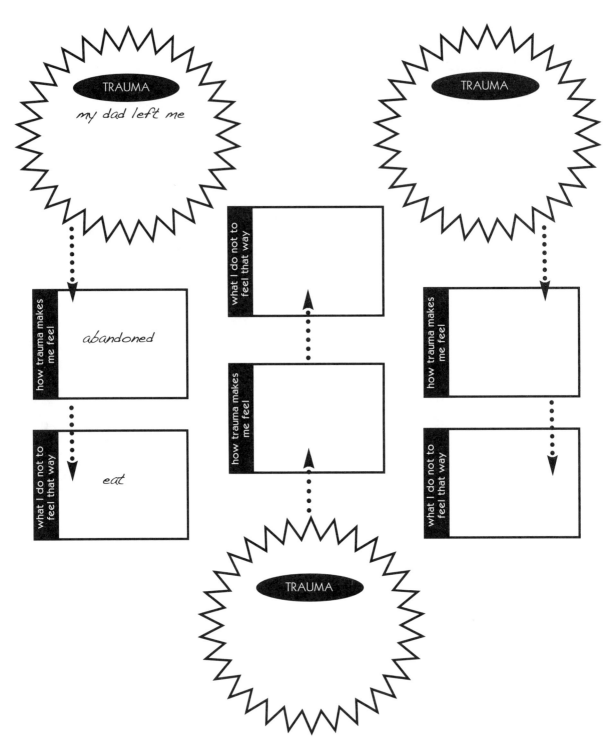

Chapter 9

The Power of Regret

For as high as the heavens are above the earth,
so great is his love for those who fear him;
as far as the east is from the west,
so far has he removed our transgressions from us.

—Psalms 103:11–12

Regret is powerful. It can overtake a mind and hold it hostage for years over lost opportunities or relationships. It can grab hold of the young and old alike and create a prison cell with no escape. Regret can rush at you with lightning speed or gradually sneak up on you like a fever. But regret can also be a very valuable tool, and how we use it for our good is what propels us toward healing.

We can only be in a prison cell of regret if we build the walls ourselves—by continually focusing on what went wrong. But there is good in every circumstance, we just need eyes to see it. There is always a bigger picture that God is working in every circumstance for our good. It's His promise.

LESSON NOTES

LESSON NOTES

Moving Through Regret

- Walk in grace. We are not perfect and we never will be. Remember we are forgiven through Christ, and when we mess up, we are able to move on.

- Accept responsibility for the choices that you've made.

- Apologize and ask forgiveness if possible.

- Look at the relationships around you. If you notice you have many regrets surrounding a certain person, maybe it's time not to be in relationship with that person.

 What are some other ways to move through regret?

Regret vs. Lessons Learned

Regret

1. I lied about who I was with and where we went the other night.

2.

3.

4.

5.

Lessons Learned

1. I broke trust and hurt people that I love.

2.

3.

4.

5.

Chapter 10

The Forgiveness Process

*Forgiveness is an act of the will,
and the will can function regardless of
the temperature of the heart.*
—Corrie Ten Boom

Forgiveness is one of the most overlooked and undervalued gifts known to mankind—possibly because many of us don't truly understand what forgiveness means. If you haven't experienced the freedom that comes after extending forgiveness, it's really difficult to communicate its full effect. I know this sounds a little cliché, but forgiveness feels like a massive stone has just rolled off your back. All the bitterness, rage, anger, and pain literally melts away. Forgiveness transforms you from a state of weakness into one of incredible strength. It takes a person with a courageous spirit and a heart of obedience toward God to forgive. It is a choice, not a feeling. Jesus commanded it for a reason.

The act of forgiveness looks different for everyone, but the process is the same. Sometimes, we have to repeat the process over and over again until it's truly complete. That's OK. The point isn't how long it takes, but that we come to the place of embracing it. Only then can we find healing; only then can we find peace and strength to move forward and let go of the past.

Sometimes we don't even recognize we haven't forgiven someone. The burden we carry without it becomes so enmeshed into who we are. That's why it's important to evaluate our hearts; to search our spirits for any hitch that causes a snag in our relationship with God and the growth and healing He wants us to have. We will soon find that not only does forgiveness release us from sin's bondage; it also connects us to Jesus in profound ways.

LESSON NOTES

LESSON NOTES

Forgiveness Process

1. Recognize the situation for what it is—someone has hurt you and it doesn't feel good.

2. Allow yourself to feel the betrayal and hurt. Allow yourself to grieve what was or what could have been.

3. Get mad. It's OK to be upset when someone hurts you. You are important and your feelings are important.

   Here is where a lot of people stop the process. They stay in the hurt and angry place. But there is not true life there.

4. Whenever you think about the situation and those angry/hurt feelings bubble up, pray. Pray, pray, pray. Cover yourself with prayer and let God take those memories and allow you to see them for what they are—memories. It's not happening now, it happened in the past. But when things aren't resolved, the feelings remain fresh.

5. Learn Bible verses that are about forgiveness and love. Put them on your bathroom mirror or on the pantry door (two places where I look the most…sadly.)

6. After a while, you will begin to notice that the memories are not in your mind as much. And when those memories do pop up, they don't have power over you like they used to. They don't have the ability to control your emotions like before. You are not so exposed to the attacks anymore; you have created a shield of prayer around you. This means you are beginning to heal.

7. Now comes the forgiving part—the part where you are able to think about what was and not feel any anger or resentment. In fact, you are able to see the good that has come out of it. And, yes, there is good in any situation for those who love God. This is the part when you are able to let it all go. It doesn't necessarily mean you don't deal with that person anymore (my ex-husband was still in my life because of the children) but it does mean that the memories or presence of your ex no longer have power over you. I actually verbalized my forgiveness out loud to Jesus. I said, "I forgive him." When you do, it's like a release valve—it opens up and all of the hurt and pain rushes out.

8. Forgiveness doesn't mean forgetting. It means that you don't allow your past to dictate your future.

9. I decided to tell my ex-husband I forgave him, but that is not everyone's story. Not everyone is able to tell those who hurt them they have forgiven them, and that's OK.

10. Forgiveness is not for the other person, its all for you…every bit of it.

 Are you holding onto bitterness, anger, or resentment in any situation in your life?

Questions About Forgiveness

1. Is there anything or anybody that can't be forgiven?

2. What if I need help with the forgiveness process?

3. How do I know if I've really forgiven someone?

4. Do I have to be in a relationship with someone who has hurt me after I've forgiven them?

5. How many times do I have to forgive someone?

6. What if they never apologized?

7. Do I have to tell them I forgave them?

Chapter 11

Creating a Support System

*And let us consider how we may spur one another on toward
love and good deeds, not giving up meeting together,
as some are in the habit of doing, but encouraging one another—
and all the more as you see the Day approaching.*

—Hebrews 10:24–25

People are created and designed to live in community. We need one another to have connection and relationship. Many times, because of our circumstances or lack of time, we neglect our basic need to be in loving community. We become isolated and alone. How sad! Our family and friends—or, as I like to call them, "our tribe"—sends life to our souls through compassion, support, and encouragement. They also provide care in practical ways through babysitting and carpooling. It's a beautiful cycle of give and take. Sometimes we give and other times we need to take.

Everything that is meant to stand needs support at some time or another. Our bodies have legs, our houses have foundations, and our spirits have Christ. If we are to get up from our struggles and move forward, we need a support system. These are the people we invite into our lives to walk alongside us toward our goals. They may be family, friends, or friends who become family. Either way, we walk together—we are a tribe.

LESSON NOTES

LESSON NOTES

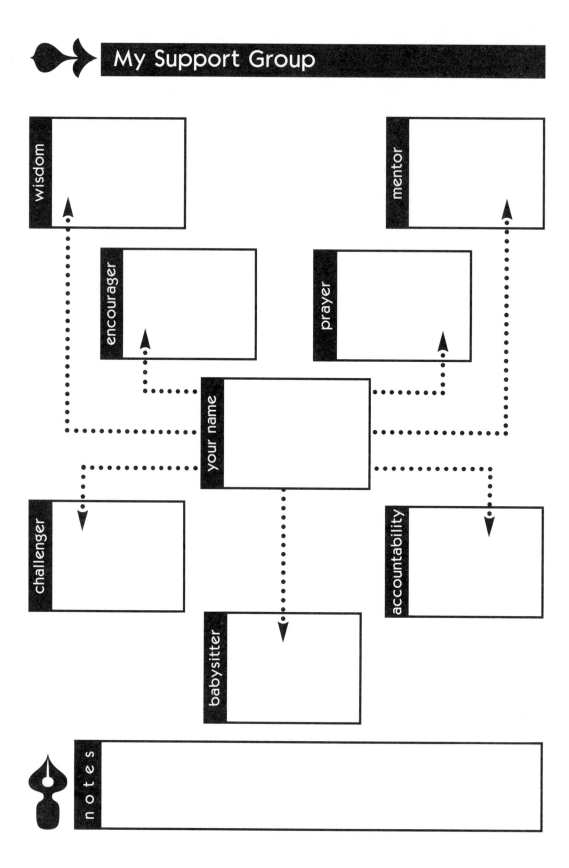

Section 3: Lesson Plans

Congratulations! You did it! You completed the *Ignite* curriculum! Now, you have hopefully gained some pretty amazing insight into your life and where you want to be in the future. I pray that you have made some new friends and feel confident about taking the next steps on your journey.

It was very important to me that each *Ignite* student workbook contain all the lesson plans and materials lists. First, I wanted the students to be able to see that each lesson was specifically designed with a clear purpose and with a focus to promote individual growth and empowerment.

Since you have taken the workshop, I truly hope you pass this information along. Get a set of workbooks, use the lessons, and start an Ignite group of your own. We need one another. We need prayer. We need guidance, and you've now got the skills to help—now it's time to pass them along! It's such a beautiful cycle of giving and receiving, paying forward, and loving our neighbor.

To order copies of *Ignite* student workbook and lesson plans visit:
www.shannondegarmo.com or Amazon.com.

If you like *Ignite*, check out *Single Moms 101: What to Know About Raising a Family on Your Own (and Then Some)* and *The Bounce Back Woman: Finding Strength Through the Ups and Downs of Life,* also written by Shannon DeGarmo.

Before the lessons begin, take time to go over the Ignite Commitment Statement with your group. It's important to create a safe atmosphere for the girls, as during this process they will be sharing some painful experiences. Laying the foundation of trust and confidentiality can better ensure a more in-depth discussion time.

How to Access the Career Personality Profiler

As part of the *Ignite* curriculum, the first lesson, Finding Strengths, contains an aptitude test called the Career Personality Profiler. It's quick and easy to take—I'm talking fifteen minutes of your time. You'll get immediate answers given in understandable vocabulary (my mind needs simple!). There are no wrong answers. They simply enable you to see what strengths you were born with (your gifts) and how you can use your God-given talents in your employment and educational choices. It's a great place to start for learning more about who you are.

I want to add that I feel very blessed that the test service, Truity, is willing to allow access to the test at discounted rates.

If you are a nonprofit organization or have 501(c)(3) status and want to implement the *Ignite* curriculum, I highly encourage you to apply for Truity's Affordable Assessment Program, which provides low- to no-cost assessments for nonprofits, charities, and schools serving people in need. The application is quick to complete. If you qualify, Truity will work out a price that fits within your budget, set you up with their testing platform, and provide ongoing support. You can find an application for this program at https://www.truity.com/content/career-assessments-charities-nonprofits-and-schools. *Do this before you begin the curriculum so you can have the tests ready for the group.*

If you are not part of a nonprofit and are completing the curriculum in your own small group, please visit https://www.truity.com/test/career-personality-profiler-test to receive ten dollars off. Once you complete the Career Personality Profiler, follow the process to purchase your full test results, and enter the coupon code IGNITE10 when prompted.

There are many aspects to self-discovery, and this is just the beginning. I'm so excited for you to take this journey!

Finding Your Strengths: Taking an Aptitude Test

Objectives:
- Understanding the importance of personal gifts
- Complete the Career Personality Profiler Test
- Analyze the results
- Discuss and decide on a plan to further future education or career choices

Materials:
- Career Personality Profiler Test
  Before the lesson, please go to https://www.truity.com/content/career-assessments-charities-nonprofits-and-schools and fill out the Affordable Assessment for Nonprofits to receive the Career Personality Profiler Test at a greatly reduced rate or free. They will then give you a link to send to the students to use for their Career Personality Profiler Test. If you are not a nonprofit, please use the discount: IGNITE10
- Computer/laptop
- Printer
- Paper/pencil
- Career/Education Mapping Sheet

Set: Read aloud Quotes of Strength:

> "If you don't like the road you're walking, start paving another one."
> —*Dolly Parton*

> "You can't give up! If you give up, you're like everybody else."
> —*Chris Evert*

> "The tests we face in life's journey are not to reveal our weaknesses, but to help us discover our inner strengths. We can only know how strong we are when we strive and thrive beyond the challenges we face."
> —*Kemi Sogunle*

> "You may encounter many defeats, but you must not be defeated. In fact, it may be necessary to encounter the defeats, so you can know who you are, what you can rise from, how you can still come out of it."
> —*Maya Angelou*

Talking Points:

- Ask students what the quotes make them think of and allow for responses. (Do the quotes have any similarities? What do the quotes make them feel?)
- Ask, "Why would someone keep trying at something when their circumstances are difficult?"
- Explain that it takes strength for someone to rise out of adversity. Ask where strength comes from with the intent to bring everyone's focus on strength that comes from the Lord. He places it inside of us. Recite Philippians 4:13: "I can do all this through him who gives me strength."
- Explain that we are all born with certain strengths and gifts. We may have to discover them and refine them, but they originate from God. Read Romans 12:6–8: "We have different gifts, according to the grace given to each of us. If your gift is prophesying, then prophesy in accordance with your faith; if it is serving, then serve; if it is teaching, then teach; if it is to encourage, then give encouragement; if it is giving, then give generously; if it is to lead, do it diligently; if it is to show mercy, do it cheerfully."
- Tell students that they probably know some of their strengths, but others are still to be discovered. Some are revealed through both adversity and struggles. Others are revealed through our passions and things we get excited about.
- We can depend on our strengths throughout our lives to help others and to push us forward.
- It's important to know what our strengths are and how we can possibly use them in a career. If we choose a career that uses our strengths, chances are we are going to enjoy that career so much more than if we don't.
- Careers don't just plop down in our laps. We must choose one and create a path to reach that goal.
- Taking an aptitude test is a great way to figure out our strengths and how they fit into educational study and then into our career paths. Give the website for taking the test.
- Allow 10–15 minutes to take the test. (Instructions are at the top.)
- Print out results for each student and allow time for them to look at their test results. Explain how to read them if needed.
- Allow for students to find others who have similar results for connection purposes.
- Throughout the upcoming lessons, when students are completing assessments, meet with each one individually to discuss their test results and help formulate a plan for moving forward.
- Use Career/Educational Mapping sheet in the workbook section to write down specific plans.

Creating a Life Mission Statement

Objectives:

- Understand the benefits of a Life Mission Statement
- Analyze personal goals and direction in life
- Create a personal Life Mission Statement

Materials:

- My Life Mission Statement sheet
- Examples of Personal Life and Biblical Mission Statements sheets
- Pen/pencil
- Paper
- White board/dry erase markers
- Art supplies (crayons, colored pencils, markers)

Set: Read aloud some examples from the Personal Life Mission Statements sheet:
- *"I define personal success as being consistent to my own personal mission statement: to love God and love others."* Joel Manby, owner of family-oriented entertainment organizations like Dollywood and Harlem Globetrotters
- *"To serve as a leader, live a balanced life, and apply ethical principles to make a significant difference."* Denise Morrison, CEO Campbell's Soup Company
- *"To glorify God by being a faithful steward of all that is entrusted to us. To have a positive influence on all who come in contact with Chick-fil-A."* Truett Cathy, founder of Chick-fil-A

Lesson:

- Ask students why personal mission statements are important and allow time for response.
- Explain (write on the board as well) that personal mission statements are:
    - an excellent way to define purpose.
    - tools to give you a strong sense of who you are.
    - to provide clear direction.
    - to form an understanding about what drives you.
- Mission statements are a "big picture" idea about who you are now and what kind of legacy you want to leave.
- Ask students to define legacy and state why it's important to leave a positive one. The goal here is to challenge everyone to be better and, hopefully, have a positive influence on those around us now for years after we are gone.

- Life mission statements can be seasonal. For example, one of my mission statements included parenting my children. Now that most of my children are adults, my mission statement has been modified to fit a new season of life.
- In creating a life mission statement, we can look at several things:
  - Look to the Bible and guidance from Jesus. We are told that we are created to glorify the Lord—"Everyone who is called by my name, whom I created for my glory, whom I formed and made" Isaiah 43:7. So, if we are walking in Christ, our mission statement should include God and His plans for us.
  - Include personal gifts. If you love to teach, serve, or volunteer, it should be part of your statement.
  - Think about your future self—who you want to be—and write something that points in that direction.
  - Include your legacy goals mentioned above. What do you want people to remember you as?

In a nutshell, a life mission statement states your purpose on this planet and how you will use your gifts that God has given you to fulfill that purpose. Goals and life decisions are filtered through your statement in order to stay on track and maintain integrity of self in the process.

- For example, one woman I knew struggled with her self-image and looked to men to make her feel valued. Her mission statement included that she would lean on God for her value and not become distracted by men. So, whenever a man would ask her out, she remembered her mission statement and found more and more value in God. (She did end up dating after a time of healing, but she re-wrote her mission statement when she knew the time was appropriate.)
- Have students take out the My Life Mission Statement sheet for creating their own mission statement. Give them a blank sheet of paper as well to write drafts. Remind them this is their mission statement for this season. They can rewrite it over time.
- Let them share with the class if time permits.

Importance of Setting Goals

Objectives:

- Understand the benefits of having personal goals
- Decide on three reachable goals
- Create a goal "road map" that is an individual plan for how to achieve set goals

Materials:

- Goal Setting and Plan Graphic Organizer
- Pen/pencil
- Paper
- Colored pencils, markers, or crayons
- White board/dry erase markers

Set: On top of a blank sheet of paper, have students write down what their age will be in five years. Then ask them to write down in a couple of sentences stating what they want to be doing by that time, either personally, spiritually, or career wise.

Lesson:

- Have students share some of their answers.
- After a time of sharing, ask students, "How are you going to make that happen?" and allow time for responses.
- Explain that seeing a bigger picture of our lives and creating a vision is important. However, it can seem overwhelming with all the work it involves. That's where personal goals come in.

Explain that:
- Setting goals is a way to become laser focused on how to achieve a purpose.
- Accomplishing goals builds self-confidence and allows us to feel successful often which breed's motivation to do even more.
- Setting goals in your mind isn't as effective because it's so easy to become distracted and get off track from a certain goal.
- Some studies show that if you set a goal and then write it down, you've just upped your chances of reaching that goal by 42 percent. (Dominican University of California study, 2016.) If you write it down and also tell someone your goal to hold you accountable, your chances of reaching that goal are even higher.
- Goals have to be attainable with a given timeline.

- Some goals may take weeks, some may take years.
- When setting a goal, it is important to make a plan to reach that goal. It's the "how" of a goal.
- It's important to understand that having too many or not enough goals won't allow you to reach your potential. I have found that having three goals at once works great, and they can be a mix of long- and short-term goals.
- Once one goal is reached, cross it off the list and write a new one in its place.

To get started:
- Write down the following goal process on the board:
  - Pray about your motives and your passions and write them down.
  - Goals should be in line with your Life Mission Statement.
  - Give yourself flexible deadlines—they are meant as a guide. As long as you are working toward your goal is what matters. If the timeline needs to be extended, that's OK. If you've reached your goal before your deadline, that's OK too.
  - Get support from people in your support system.
  - Always add a new goal when an old one is reached.
  - Use phrases like "I will" or "I want," not "I wish" or "I hope."
  - Create a plan on how to achieve each goal.

- Explain that the students are going to be writing their own goals, and have them take out a blank sheet of paper. Have them write down things they are passionate about, things they care about, and their hopes and dreams. Encourage the students to fill the page.
- When it seems most students are done, have them organize their paper according to items that are in common by circling those items in the same color. For example, if someone wrote family, children, and parenting on their sheet, they can circle those in yellow. If they also wrote getting a degree, going to school, and getting good grades, they can circle those in blue.
- When they are done organizing their paper into color-coded groups, have them categorize their groups: Family, Education, Financial, Spiritual, etc. Then have them begin thinking about goals for each category and write them down on another sheet of paper. Example: I want to be a better mom. I want to get a good job. I want to get my high school diploma. This list can be as long as they want and as simple or complex as they want.
- Explain that it's OK, even normal, if they are starting to feel overwhelmed. It's a lot of stuff, but you are going to help them prioritize everything and list how it will get done in small increments so it will feel manageable.

- When they are finished categorizing, instruct them to look at their goals and begin to prioritize them for each group. Determine which one is most urgent, and so forth. For example, if you want a decent paying job, you must first complete high school (if they haven't already), then possibly pursue higher education. It must be in step-by-step order.

Now it's time for the Goal Setting and Plan Graphic Organizer:
- Have students choose their top three goals to work toward within the next six months. This doesn't mean they will achieve them (although it can be something to achieve), it means they can *begin* to achieve them. For example, if someone wants to get her cosmetology degree, she can begin the work, even though it will take longer than six months to achieve. That's OK.
- Then have them write out their goals and plans on the Goal Setting Graphic Organizer.
- Remind them *they are now 42 percent more likely to achieve since they just wrote it down!*
- Remind them of their support system and their accountability partners.
- Go over some of their goals with them.
- If you wonder if they are challenging enough, encourage them to push themselves a bit more. If you feel they seem too challenging to start with, help them find a goal or two that will make them feel successful sooner.
- Remind students that once a goal is achieved, cross it out and remember to celebrate—it's a big deal! Then put a new goal down from the longer list they've already created.

Writing a Résumé

Objectives:

- Become familiar with the different parts of a résumé and the overall goal in writing one
- Identify personal skills and past experiences to include
- Create a rough draft and, ultimately, a final document

Materials:

- Paper/pencil
- Create Your Own Résumé template
- Shannon DeGarmo example résumé
- Résumé Rules

Set: Using a photo, either printed or a digital one on your phone, show a picture of someone. It doesn't matter who it is, just as long as the photo is clear. Then have the class describe the physical attributes of him or her.

Next ask them to state the person's possible strengths and weaknesses. You may have some wild guesses, but obviously they won't know any. This helps define the point of a resume: to let others know who the person is behind the face.

Lesson:

- Explain that in the job world, résumés are to give an inside glimpse of our strengths and weaknesses to a potential employer. They provide information about a person in a quick and efficient way. Think of it as a "written selfie."
- The goal of a résumé is to grab the employer's attention, so they'll want to meet for an interview.
- Stress that their résumé needs to be unique with a splash of personality, be easy to read, and clearly convey the value someone brings to the job they're applying for.
- State that sometimes, writing a résumé can be overwhelming, especially if they feel they don't have a lot of skills to offer, but that's OK! Most people don't realize just how much they've done until they sit and write it down.
- Before getting started, review and discuss the Résumé Rules:
  - Always add contact information at the top of the front page. How else will an employer know how to connect for an interview?
  - Don't lie—it's *never* okay to lie. Employers run background checks and call references. Lying is the quickest and best way never to get hired.

- Don't include any unnecessary information like marital status, hobbies (unless one relates to the job), or social media tags. Employers will have already looked up their social media. On that note, make sure their media posts have appropriate language, photos, and absolutely no political references.
- Do not mention salary expectations—money is to be discussed in an interview.
- Don't complain about a former employer. It puts *them* in a bad light and could possibly make a future employer nervous about hiring them.
- Create a professional email address. Professional email addresses usually include first and last name (or last initial). Iheartcats@gmail.com is not a professional email address!
- Always have a good friend look it over to check for grammar and spelling errors. Plus, let them give honest feedback—they may think of something that got missed, or they may have a great idea to include.
- After discussing the Résumé Rules, look at an example of a completed résumé. You can either use your own or use mine (see the Shannon DeGarmo example). Review the key points that are included to give an overall view.

Now it's time to pull out the Create Your Own Résumé template:
- First, explain that they can use the template to apply for a pretend job, or if they already have a real job to apply for, it could be used as a rough draft. Whatever they do, they will need to type in their own information, and try to keep it on one page.
- Note that the contact information goes first. Also discuss putting a short quote afterward to help communicate a deeper personal passion right off the bat. It's a perfect attention grabber and way to get the employer to remember them. Students can use their phones to find one.

Proceed to explain and discuss the different sections:
- **Career Objective:**
  - Since there could be several positions open at the same company, the objective communicates exactly what position they are applying for. For example, if they are applying for a bank teller position, then the objective could read: Motivated individual seeking to fill a teller position at "Such and Such" bank.
- **Education:**
  - This section communicates their educational background, including any classes taken and certificates received from a trade school or

community center. If they are continuing a degree, then they need to put that down. All schools (high school and up) need to be listed along with any achievements made, including extra-curricular activities they were recognized for.

- **Employment History:**
  - Starting with the most recent jobs, list the main responsibilities performed and the beginning and end dates they were there. If they don't know exact dates, then put down months and years. NOTE: Don't say why they left each job. That can be explained in the interview.
  - If you find that someone lists a lot of jobs for a short amount of time, then only put down the ones they had the longest and are the most recent. If there was a life circumstance (a pregnancy, a trauma, an addiction) that kept them from maintaining a job, have them prepare to explain that in the interview.
- **Skills and Interests:**
  - Explain that this is a short, bulleted list that shows them off. It is to briefly describe what skills they have and how they come together to make a well-rounded person who is qualified for the position.
  - Have students brainstorm skills out loud with the class. That way, students can play off each other's strengths and ideas to add to their own lists. Ask them to put five to ten skills and no more than two interests.
- **References:**
  - Discuss the importance of having at least three positive references. These are people who are not related but who know them well enough to boast about strong character and work ethics. Be sure the people they list have given their permission to use them, so they are prepared when they get a call from an employer.
  - Stress for them to include a couple of people they've worked with, a reference from a former employer, and a reference from a family friend.

After the rough draft is complete, encourage each student to take it home, type it out, and save it. Whenever they have a new job experience, gain a new skill, or complete a class or degree, they can add it on to their résumé. It should be a fluid (ever changing) document.

Getting a Job

Objectives:

- Learn basic job interview etiquette
- Learn appropriate job interview attire
- Learn how to properly give a handshake
- Discuss personal responses to job interview questions
- Participate in mock job interview

Materials:

- Handshake Rules sheet
- Do's and Don'ts Attire sheet
- Mock Job Interview sheet
- Index cards

Set: Choose a volunteer, have them walk up to you, and hold out your hand to shake theirs. Introduce yourself.

Lesson:

Start by asking students why handshakes are important. Explain it's the very first type of communication we give to a possible new employer.
- According to Fortune 500, if an employer were to choose between two qualified people for a job, they would choose the one with the better handshake.
- Handshakes communicate confidence, ability, and connection—or the lack of.
- Explain that body language in job interviews is very important. People will judge your character within the first couple of minutes, and a handshake is a big part of that.

Have students refer to Handshake Rules (included) and review together:
- Handshakes are with the right hand unless there is a disability.
- If you are about to meet someone, make sure your right hand is free. So if they are carrying a folder, put it in their left hand.
- Walk up to the interviewer with hands exposed (it expresses openness), not in their pockets.
- Be sure to make solid eye contact while reaching out to shake.
- The handshake should be firm (or as firm as the other person's).
- Shake hands up and down two to three times.
- Express a greeting such as "Hello," or "Good afternoon" with a smile.

- Introduce yourself by giving your first name.
- Say "It's nice to meet you," or "Thank you for having me."
- If you are sitting when someone comes into the room, stand up to shake hands.
- Things to avoid: the Dead Fish Handshake (give them an example of what that is . . . a loose, powerless handshake)

Class Exercise:

Have students find a partner to practice with.
- After the students have practiced, talk about the importance of a strong job interview. Begin by asking them to share some job interview experiences and how they felt about them.
- Explain that participating in job interviews is a skill that gets better with practice, so that's what you're all going to do.
  - The first thing to do is think about what they'll want to say to a potential employer.
  - Ask students to refer to their Personal Interview Response (PIR) portion at the top of their Mock Job Interview sheet. They can do this together to hear one another's responses.
- After everyone's PIR sheet is completed, prepare for a mock job interview. Begin by reviewing the importance of appropriate attire. First ask them what they think is appropriate. Then go over the Do's and Don'ts Attire sheet.
- Explain that before any job interview, their cell phones must be silenced and put away. Not on vibrate, but on silent.

Mock Job Interview:
- Have the students choose a partner. One will be the potential employer and the other, the applicant.
- Using the Mock Job Interview questions, have the potential employer ask five questions from the list. Then on the index cards, have the interviewer rate the responses of the applicant on a scale of 1–5 (1 being lowest and 5 being highest) and why they gave them that response. *It's always good to have *one* thing positive to say about someone when being rated.
- Explain that their responses need to be honest so everyone can learn and grow.
- When the interview is over, the partners are to switch roles and do it again.
- When the entire process is over, the partners give each other their cards so they can see their ratings and feedback.

The Meaning of Sacrifice: Needs vs. Wants

Objectives:

- Distinguish between a need and a want
- Analyze personal spending habits
- Create a personal budget

Materials:

- Everyday Life sheet
- Needs List sheet
- Budget Analyzer sheet
- This or That sheet
- Budget Balancer sheet
- Colored pencils/crayons
- Pencil/pen

Set: Have students turn to their Everyday Life sheet. Instruct them to circle the things that they need on a regular basis—that means things or services used at least two to three times per month. After they finish circling, ask them to use a colored pencil or crayon and lightly color in the things they must have to live. Discuss the results as a class.

Lesson:

- Ask students the difference between a need and a want.
    - A *need* is something we need to survive (housing, clothing, food). It is something we must have.
    - A *want* is something we would like to have.
    - Have them refer back to their Everyday Life sheet and ask if everything they circled is in fact a need.
    - Acknowledge that many of us think we need things, but we really don't.
    - Ask students to give examples of things we call needs that are really wants.
- Explain how we waste hard-earned money on things we want instead of things we need—the newest cell phone, getting highlights in our hair, gel nails, eating out—when in reality that money could be used for true needs—bills, school, diapers, doctor visits, and more. **Refer to the Needs List sheet of the reality of needs.
- Stress that it's hard to sacrifice things we want for things we need. But when working toward an educational or career goal, the sacrifices are very short lived when looking at the bigger picture.

Before looking at sacrifices, they've got to figure out where their money is going.
- As a class, have everyone review the Budget Analyzer sheet together. Then have them fill theirs out individually.
- If students don't know how much income they have, explain that is the first step to making a budget. Tell them to guess at a number to complete the activity.
- Have students fill in the blanks according to their personal budget.
- Then, have students share if their budget works for them in a way that they can save money, have an emergency fund, and work toward their goals.

Now it's time to find some ways to sacrifice and save. Stress that they may not be as drastic as they think.
- Sacrificing doesn't mean you can't do anything fun, it just means you do things differently or not as often.
- To help discover ways to trim the budget, have everyone look at the "This or That" sheet and review the directions.
- Students are to choose three wants to participate in, but in a different way that costs less. For example, instead of getting their hair highlighted at the salon (This), they can go to a beauty school and get it done cheaply or do it herself (That).
- Allow time to complete the exercise and share. They may get some great ideas from each other.

Now that students know where their money is going and how to save, it's time to make a balanced budget.
- A balanced budget is exactly what it sounds like: a way to track spending so you don't spend more than you make. Ideally, you can see how your needs will be met and how much you can save.
- Review Budget Balancer sheet instructions and allow everyone to fill theirs out. Instruct them to keep items that are needs, and if they can't find a better way to save on the wants, then maybe it becomes a sacrifice for the time being.
- Ask students to give examples from their budgets (not numbers) of what possible sacrifices could be.
- Also, encourage students to save some money in order to give. It's healthy and rewarding to give to others with their time and money, even if it's only a little bit. It's also a good reminder that the world does not revolve around our problems and us.

Who Am I? : Exploring Self-Worth

Objectives:

- Identify positive self-worth statements vs. negative self-harm statements
- Analyze self-worth from a personal perspective
- Learn how to use positive affirmation statements
- Explore how we allow others to influence our self-worth
- Understand that self-worth is given to us by God

Materials:

- Mirror (or anything that shows reflection, i.e. cell phone)
- I Am Scripture References sheets
- I Am sheet
- Markers/crayons, scissors, and glue
- Post-its
- White board

Set: First look at your own reflection in front of the class. Discuss out loud what you see regarding your physical traits. Maybe your hair roots are showing, or your skin is broken out. Then take a deeper, longer look. Ask not "What do I look like?" but "*Who am I?*" Discuss who you are on the inside—giving, friendly, organized. Maybe a little proud, guarded, sometimes absent minded. Be transparent with the students.

Allow time for students to do their own self-assessment with their reflection.

Lesson:

- Ask "Where do we get our perception of what we are worth?"
- Allow time for student discussion, and write answers on the board. They should include parents, siblings, boyfriends, friends, TV, social media, etc.
- Make the point that sometimes, after making a poor choice or having a negative experience, our perceptions get warped. We label ourselves as irresponsible or a failure rather than someone who failed because of a poor decision.
- Discuss the danger of labeling ourselves (and others). If we aren't careful, we can carry those labels around like a backpack of rocks. And they get heavy fast.
- Explain to students that the list on the board has one very major common thread: they are people filled with opinions—and opinions can be wrong, and they can change. This makes it dangerous to allow just anyone to affect our self-worth because it's not possible to please everyone all the time. None of us will ever measure up to perfection. When we try, we end up comparing

our ability to an impossible standard, which leads to feelings of defeat time and time again.
- Explain that having a negative view of self-worth will affect our mood, confidence level, and our overall happiness.
- We can only count on one thing to be a consistent, truthful reminder of our value: God. He not only created us, He has an important purpose for each one of us. He loves us so much, He died for us. He is our Father, and nothing will separate us from His love.
- If we look to God for our value, we don't have to impress, feel guilty, compare, or worry about not measuring up. Ever.

Class exercise:
- Have everyone take out their Post-its.
- Ask students to write down all the characteristics they've thought about themselves (and still do). Have them write any labels they've given themselves. Model this for the students with your own experience of harmful labels in your own life.
- Have the girls stick the post-its on themselves.
- Let them look at one another. Let them see what others think about themselves—that everybody struggles with a negative self-view. Let them realize and acknowledge they are not alone in thinking negative thoughts.
- **If a time allows, allow the girls to stand one at a time and remove their negative labels and put on new positive ones. If the class size is too big, break them into small groups.
- Example:

- Read scripture over them that combats their particular labels (see Scripture Reference sheets).
- Acknowledge that we are all works in progress. *Our choices don't define us, and our past doesn't dictate our future.* Only God has the power to do either. He alone made us and calls us His own. He has a specific purpose for us, and He will help us to fulfill it. Our true worth is great through His doing.

Have everyone throw away their negative labels and transition into affirmation self-assessment.
- Define affirmation: a positive statement that can overcome negative thoughts.

- Emphasize that a thought is just a thought—it isn't necessarily truth. Just as our minds have been conditioned to think negatively about ourselves, we can train your mind to think positively.
- Explain that in writing an affirmation, we never use the word "no" or "not"… even if we are trying to develop a particular skill.
  - Example: I'm not good at public speaking (not affirming) vs. I am working on speaking in public (affirming).
  - Example: I'm not pretty enough to have a boyfriend (not affirming) vs. I am beautifully and wonderfully made (affirming).
- Seeing ourselves in a positive light is powerful. It helps with healthy self-esteem, goal reaching, and overall contentment and joy.

Take out the I Am sheet, and explain to students they are going to write down who they are in an affirming way. For example, I Am: a work in progress; I Am: trying; I Am: funny.
- Allow time for students to begin filling out their own. Encourage them to be creative and to have fun with it. Remind the students to look at their scripture references to remind them of their worth.
- Remind the girls to keep their sheet where they can see it every day, so if or when they begin to think negatively, they are reminded of who they really are.

Identifying Coping Strategies

Objective:

- Identify how trauma causes an effect on our lives
- Analyze personal feelings around trauma
- Identify individual coping mechanisms and their effect on our lives
- Understand the difference between healthy and unhealthy coping strategies

Materials:

- Identifying Coping Strategies sheet
- Pen/pencil
- Paper or poster board
- White board

Set: Write Tim Keller quote on the board: "To be loved but not known is comforting but superficial. To be known and not loved is our greatest fear. But to be fully known and truly loved is, well, a lot like being loved by God. It is what we need more than anything. It liberates us from pretense, humbles us out of our self-righteousness, and fortifies us for any difficulty life can throw at us."

Ask students what the quote means. Why is being loved and not known comforting but superficial? What is an example? Why is being known and not loved a greatest fear? How can we fully know and love ourselves? What does that look like?

Lesson:

- Ask students to define trauma in their own words. Leave time for personal responses.
- The online definition of trauma is:
  - 1. a deeply distressing or disturbing experience;
  - 2. emotional shock following a stressful event or a physical injury, which may be associated with physical shock and sometimes, leads to long-term neurosis.
- Draw three columns on the board and label them Emotional, Physical, Both. Take time to discuss that trauma can be emotional, physical, or both. Ask them to give examples and write them under each appropriate column. Discuss examples of each.
  - Emotional trauma: unplanned pregnancy, verbal abuse, neglect, abandonment—anything that causes harm to your emotional state.

- Physical trauma: car accident, burns from a fire, and physical abuse—anything that causes harm to your physical body.
- Both physical and emotional: sexual abuse, physical abuse, rape.

Coping Mechanisms:

Because traumas are stressful, we develop coping mechanisms to help ease the pain caused by that stress. They are our way of trying to feel better about the situation whether it's current or in our past.

A few things to note:
- Sometimes we are aware of how we cope, and other times we are not.
- Some coping mechanisms are healthy and others are not.
- To truly know why we do what we do, we must understand what started the behavior in the first place.

Ask if anyone has ever said, "I know I shouldn't do this, but I can't seem to help it. Why do I keep doing it?!" We are going to answer that question today.

Read aloud: "Now we see only an indistinct image in a mirror, but then we will be face to face. Now what I know is incomplete, but then I will know fully, even as I have been fully known" 1 Corinthians 13:12 isv.

- State that we are already fully known by God, but to move forward with healing, we must fully know ourselves and why we do what we do.
- The first step is acknowledging our own behaviors, accepting responsibility for them, and determine if they're healthy or unhealthy.
- Have everyone take out the Identifying Coping Strategies sheet and fill it out. (Have more sheets of paper available since there could be students with more than one trauma). Do this exercise with them and allow students to see you fill in your blanks. Discuss with them your trauma to whatever degree you are comfortable. Tell them how it's made you feel and how you have coped.
- When the students are done, ask if any are willing to share. Emphasize that they are in a safe place where there is no judgment.
- Write down coping mechanisms on the board as the students identify them.
- After you're finished, make two columns on the board: Healthy and Unhealthy. Leave a space between the columns.
- Allow the students to label the strategies. For example, a healthy coping mechanism may be to take a run. However, if you start to run all the time and it becomes an addiction to running, weight loss, and outward appearance, it can turn into an unhealthy mechanism.

- Allow time for students to brain storm more healthy coping mechanisms that are not listed. Good examples are praying, journaling, any form of expression such as painting, singing, playing music, drawing, sewing, anything creative.
- Encourage students to continue identify more coping behaviors at home.

The Power of Regret

Objectives:
- Define regret
- Identify regret as a valuable tool
- Analyze personal regret
- Acknowledge what personal opportunities are born from regret

Materials:
- Regret vs. Lessons Learned sheet
- Pen/pencil

Set: Write this verse on the board: "For godly grief produces a repentance that leads to salvation without regret, whereas worldly grief produces death" 2 Corinthians 7:10.
- Ask students what this means in their own words.
- Explain that "godly grief" is a deep sorrow of the heart that comes with true repentance of a particular sin. It is grief that brings a change of heart and actions, and it leads to a greater intimacy with Jesus as a result. In short, we are very sorry, and we will never do it again. There is no room for regret in godly grief because we are made new—our slate is clean for a fresh start, and we can walk in freedom from that sin.
- Then define "worldly grief": it's when we are sorry that we got caught. The behavior doesn't change (at least not for long), and there is no real repentance. It brings death because we remain in the same state of disobedience, which means separation from God. Our heart remains in the ways of the world rather than in Jesus.

Lesson:
- Ask students what they think regret means.
- Merriam-Webster's dictionary definition defines regret as two different meanings and parts of speech.
  - (verb): *to be very sorry for*. An example: She regretted the words that came out of her mouth.
  - (noun): *sorrow aroused by circumstances beyond one's control or power to repair* or *an expression of distressing emotion* (such as sorrow).
- Briefly share with the class a time when you felt regret.
- Ask a few students to share a time when they felt regretful about something.

- Ignite answers by explaining that a regret can be the way they behaved, things they've said or done, and things they would do differently if given the chance.
- Ask if everyone agrees that regret is a very powerful emotion. Share that some studies show that regret can be more powerful than anger, guilt, sadness, and even pride (or feeling proud about something).
- Explain that there are two types of regret: 1. regret over a missed opportunity (such as not taking a job or going on a trip); and 2. the regret of making a poor choice (such as doing something you know you shouldn't have).
- Ask: How can regret be a valuable emotion if it feels so bad? Explain that it is valuable because regret presents new opportunity to learn and make better choices moving forward. So instead of focusing on the negative outcome now, focus on a brighter future because of the lesson learned. In a nutshell, the lessons we learn and carry with us help us construct better choices in our future.

  **NOTE: If we don't reflect on our regret and what we could or should have done differently, we won't be able to recognize the lessons that can come from it. But reflecting and dwelling are different. Dwelling on regrets (for days, months, even a lifetime) leads to beating ourselves down and feeling defeated. Reflecting is short-term and sets us up for victory in our future.

Take out Regret vs. Lessons Learned sheet.
- Ask the class to think about some regrets they have and write them down in the appropriate space. Then have them write down the lesson(s) they learned from each one.
- Encourage students to share their answers.
- Then have girls rip their papers down the middle vertically so one piece has the regrets and the other has the list of lessons. Have them wad up and throw away the list of regrets and keep the list of lessons learned.
- State that, to really move forward, we need to focus on what we've learned.

Now explain that there are other important ways to move through regret. Refer to the Moving Through Regret page in the workbook.
- Give grace to yourself. You are not perfect, and you never will be. Jesus wants you to walk in His grace.
- Remember that you are forgiven through Christ, and when you mess up, you can move on without the burden or weight of guilt—He has taken it upon Himself to carry.

- Accept responsibility for the consequences of your choices. Doing so shows your character and builds integrity.
- Apologize and ask forgiveness if at all possible. (Don't worry about the other person's response. Your part is to seek it.)
- Look at the relationships around you. If you notice you have regrets involving a certain person, it's probably time not to be in relationship with him or her.

The Forgiveness Process

Objectives:

- Identify any pain and resentment
- Understand what forgiveness is and its purpose
- Identify any people and circumstances that forgiveness is being withheld
- Begin the forgiveness process

Materials:

- Paper/pencil
- White board/markers
- Forgiveness Process sheet
- Questions About Forgiveness sheet cut into strips and passed out among the class. Cut strips out before lesson so they are ready to be passed out.

Set: Write this quote on the board: "As I walked out the door toward the gate that would lead to my freedom, I knew if I didn't leave my bitterness and hatred behind, I'd still be in prison."—Nelson Mandela

Lesson:

- Discuss with students the meaning of the Mandela quote, and allow for responses. Expound on the point that if we carry bitterness from pain that others have caused, we remain in a prison-type state of mind.
- Unforgiveness holds us captive to our pain. It colors our choices, our attitudes, and our connections toward others, and it hinders us from moving toward healing and freedom.
- Holding on to pain and resentment actually can have physical effects too:
  - Higher levels of anxiety
  - Insomnia
  - Depression
  - PTSD symptoms
- Express that we've all had painful seasons, sometimes even decades, in our lives.
- Ask "How do we move on from the desert place of pain toward forgiveness?" and allow for answers.
- Ask "Do we forgive just because it's good for our health?" and allow for answers. Touch on the truth that, while forgiveness does bring health benefits, the core reason we extend it is because Christ tells us to. "Get rid of all bitterness, rage and anger, brawling and slander, along with every form of

malice. Be kind and compassionate to one another, forgiving each other, just as in Christ God forgave you" Ephesians 4:31–32.
- Christ tells us to forgive because He knows we won't ever feel like doing it on our own. He knows that, through forgiveness, our spirits are healed and set free. He knows the anchor—the weight—that bitterness carries, and He wants us free of that burden.
- State that if we want a life of healthy connections and full relationships, we must forgive.

Forgiveness Is a Process:

- Discuss with the group: Forgiveness is a process, and everyone's can look a little different. Some people take a long time to forgive, and others are able to work through it quickly. What's important to remember is, it's your process, and how you do it and when is up to you. Just as long as you do it.
- Have everyone reference The Forgiveness Process in the workbook.
- Go over the process together. Allow time for responses.
- After the process has been discussed, pass out Questions About Forgiveness strips to random students:
  – Allow those who have questions to read out loud, and allow students to discuss answers as a class.
  – Then guide them with the answers provided with the strips.

  Answers to Questions About Forgiveness Strips:

  1. Is there anybody or anything that can't be forgiven?
     Answer: There is only one unforgiveable sin, *"Truly I tell you, people can be forgiven all their sins and every slander they utter, but whoever blasphemes against the Holy Spirit will never be forgiven; they are guilty of an eternal sin." Matthew 3:28-29* Many believe that means anyone who rejects the Holy Spirit (who chooses not to believe in Jesus) is committing the unforgiveable sin because they are refusing salvation. However, if we are in Christ, we have been forgiven and in turn are called to forgive others. *Bear with each other and forgive one another if any of you has a grievance against someone. Forgive as the Lord forgave you. Colossians 3:13* There are no stipulations here. We are called to forgive anything and everything because the Lord has forgiven us.

  2. What if I need help in my forgiveness process?
     Answer: That's okay! We all need someone to walk alongside of us and encourage us to do what the Lord calls us to do. Talk to a Christian counselor, a trusted friend or mentor who will guide you with loving patience and encourage you towards forgiveness.

3. How do I know if I've really forgiven someone?

    Answer: The answer truly is: you know when you know. Many believe forgiveness is a release of anger, resentment and pain about a situation and the one who offended you. When you are able to see the offender as a human being with hurts and brokenness, and be able to feel compassion for someone who has hurt you. It's releasing that "offender" to God and allowing Him to deal with the situation, instead of you trying to get revenge. It's freedom from a circumstance instead of having feelings of rage and bitterness attached to it.

4. Do I have to be in relationship with someone who has hurt me after I've forgiven them?

    Answer: This is a tricky one. Forgiveness doesn't necessarily mean reconciliation. So it is up to you to evaluate your relationship to see if you want to continue or not. But, if your offender is an ex-husband or boyfriend who you share child custody arrangements with, or if that person is a parent or sibling it can be difficult to sever all relational ties with them. Any relationship you choose to be in should be safe and healthy. If that isn't possible due to circumstances in the relationship seek a counselor as to find best ways to communicate with those who need to be communicated with, but at the same time, keep you safe in the relationship.

5. How many times do I have to forgive someone?

    Answer: The answer is pretty simple. We forgive someone an infinite number of times. *"Then Peter came to Jesus and asked, "Lord, how many times shall I forgive my brother or sister who sins against me? Up to seven times?" Jesus answered, "I tell you, not seven times, but seventy-seven times." Matthew 18:21-22.* However, if you are continually having to forgive someone over and over again because they continually hurt you in the your relationship, it would be good to be reflective to see if this relationship is healthy and one you need to continue being in.

6. What if they never apologized?

    Answer: Forgiveness is not for the "offender" it is for the "offended." We are called to forgive. Not because the offender has apologized, but because Christ has forgiven us.

7. Do I have to tell them I forgave them?

    Answer: That all depends on you and how you feel the Lord leading you. Some people feel led to express their forgiveness. Some feel like it is unsafe to express their forgiveness because of past abuse in the relationship. Others can't express their forgiveness because of death or abandonment of the offender. Pray about the next step in your personal forgiveness journey, and see how the Lord is guiding you.

- Allow for a five-minute quiet time for reflection so students can examine their hearts and see if there is any bitterness they are harboring. One sure way to know is when they think of a certain person, they feel immediate anger or pain.
• Challenge students to begin the process of forgiveness so they can be set free.

Creating a Support System

Objectives:
- Identify qualities of good friendships
- Understand that balance is important in friendship
- Identify qualities of those in a support system
- Identify the benefits of a support system
- Create a usable support system

Materials:
- My Support Group sheet
- Pen/pencil
- Post-its
- White Board/dry erase markers
- Six to seven small books for the class exercise

Set: Write on the board, "What does, 'If you want a friend, you have to be a friend.' Mean?" Allow time for responses.

Lesson:
- Discuss how friends are an important part of life. They can help through depression, increase happiness, improve self-confidence, help fight stress from trauma, help achieve goals, and according to the Mayo Clinic, friends even help lower your body mass index (BMI).
- Explain that, when choosing friends, it's important to remember that the quality of friend is much more important than the number you have.

Design a Friend:
- Draw a stick figure of a "friend" on the board, and tell them we are going to make the perfect friend.
- Have students write one or two of the most important qualities they think are important in a friendship on a post-it and have them stick it on the white board.
- Read them aloud for the class to hear.
- Expound on the virtues that are strong character qualities. If some are not, then explain why. For example, popularity, having money, or driving a nice car are not examples of character qualities.
- Continue to add to the list on the board if there are not any strong qualities listed that are found in a true friend, such as: trustworthy, open

communication, secure, honest, commonly accepted values, dependable, encouraging.
- Ask students if they see these qualities in themselves—are they the kind of friend they expect their friends to be?

Class Exercise:
- Ask a volunteer to stand at the front of the class and hold their hands straight out to their sides, like a balanced scale.
- Discuss what balance looks like in a friendship. State that if one person is always calling, if one person is always listening, if one person is always giving or sacrificing, the friendship can get off balance. Each time you say "listening," "giving," "sacrificing," "calling," place a book on one of the volunteer's hand so she looks off balance.
- Explain that friendships need balance to be strong and healthy. There needs to be give-and-take from each person.
- Then place a couple of books in the other hand to show better balance.

Identifying Unbalanced Friendships:
- Ask, "What are symptoms of an unhealthy friendship?" and allow for answers. Examples might include: you feel pulled down when they're around; you get into trouble when you're together; they lie or you find yourself lying for them; they suck energy out of you; you feel exhausted.
- State that oftentimes unhealthy friendships need to end, especially when we are struggling as it is . . . and that's OK.
- Tell a time when a friendship ended for you and why it was a good thing.
- Allow students to express a time when a friendship of theirs ended.
- Explain that some friends are friends for life and others are for a season. It all depends on the value of the friendship and the circumstances when you know them.
- Explain that developing good, positive friendships is important when moving forward in personal growth. We need friends who will encourage, even help us to meet our goals.

Support Systems:
- Having a network of people around us who are around to encourage and are willing to help us is called a support system.
- Explain that some people are born into good support systems (i.e. strong family ties), but others have to create their own, and that works too. Most people have a mixture of both.

- Explain that different people we choose in our support system will fill different roles. One may be an encourager and prayer partner, but not great at babysitting. Another may be a great babysitter, but not the best for homework support. What's important is, each one needs to know that they are part of your support system and, in turn, you are willing to support them however you can. That way there is balance—it's a give/take relationship.

Creating a Support System:
- In creating a support system, there needs to be someone for each of the following roles (write these on the board):
  - Wisdom
  - A mentor (for career and educational guidance)
  - Encouragement
  - Prayer
  - A challenger—someone who will be honest with you about your behavior and choices
  - An accountability partner—someone who will intentionally check in with you on your progress toward your goals
  - A babysitter
- State that they may not find someone to fill all of these roles, but it is possible. It just takes time.
- Remind students that in order to have a friend in a support system, they need to be willing to support someone else as well.
- It's important to note: If a "friend" has shown abusive tendencies toward them in the past, they do not qualify for or belong in their support system. The people they choose must be positive, encouraging, and safe.
- Acknowledge that some students in the class could be part of their support system.
- Express the importance of telling those in their support system what their role is, and that your relationship goes beyond just a regular friendship. It's an honor to be part of a support system.
- Using the My Support Group sheet, write down examples of your personal support system.
- Allow time for students to fill out their My Support Group sheet.
- Tell students to put it in a place where they can see it often. That way, they have a visual for showing that they are not alone—they are supported.